What Did You Do Yesterday?

Jacqueline Martin

T0346727

Name _____

Age _____

Class _____

OXFORD
UNIVERSITY PRESS

OXFORD
UNIVERSITY PRESS

Great Clarendon Street, Oxford OX2 6DP

Oxford University Press is a department of the University of Oxford.
It furthers the University's objective of excellence in research, scholarship,
and education by publishing worldwide in

Oxford New York

Auckland Cape Town Dar es Salaam Hong Kong Karachi
Kuala Lumpur Madrid Melbourne Mexico City Nairobi
New Delhi Shanghai Taipei Toronto

With offices in

Argentina Austria Brazil Chile Czech Republic France Greece
Guatemala Hungary Italy Japan South Korea Poland Portugal
Singapore Switzerland Thailand Turkey Ukraine Vietnam

OXFORD and OXFORD ENGLISH are registered trade marks of
Oxford University Press in the UK and in certain other countries

© Oxford University Press 2005

The moral rights of the author have been asserted

Database right Oxford University Press (maker)

First published 2005

2023

26

No unauthorized photocopying

All rights reserved. No part of this publication may be reproduced,
stored in a retrieval system, or transmitted, in any form or by any means,
without the prior permission in writing of Oxford University Press,
or as expressly permitted by law, or under terms agreed with the appropriate
reprographics rights organization. Enquiries concerning reproduction
outside the scope of the above should be sent to the ELT Rights Department,
Oxford University Press, at the address above

You must not circulate this book in any other binding or cover
and you must impose this same condition on any acquirer

Any websites referred to in this publication are in the public domain and
their addresses are provided by Oxford University Press for information only.
Oxford University Press disclaims any responsibility for the content

ISBN: 978 0 19 440100 5

Printed in China

Illustrations by: Andy Hamilton

With thanks to Sally Spray for her contribution to this series

Reading Dolphins
Notes for teachers & parents

📖 Using the book

1 Begin by looking at the first story page (page 2). Look at the picture and ask questions about it. Then read the story text under the picture with your students. Use section 1 of the CD for this if possible.

2 Teach and check the understanding of any new vocabulary. Note that some of the words are in the **Picture Dictionary** at the back of the book.

3 Now look at the activities on the right-hand page. Show the example to the students and instruct them to complete the activities. This may be done individually, in pairs, or as a class.

4 Do the same for the remaining pages of the book.

5 Retell the whole story more quickly, reinforcing the new vocabulary. Section 2 of the CD can help with this.

6 If possible, listen to the expanded story (section 3 of the CD). The students should follow in their books.

7 When the book is finished, use the **Picture Dictionary** to check that students understand and remember new vocabulary. Section 4 of the CD can help with this.

💿 Using the CD

The CD contains four sections.

1 The story told slowly, with pauses. Use this during the first reading. It may also be used for "Listen and repeat" activities at any point.

2 The story told at normal speed. This should be used once the students have read the book for the first time.

3 The expanded story. The story is told in a longer version. This will help the students understand English when it is spoken faster, as they will now know the story and the vocabulary.

4 Vocabulary. Each word in the **Picture Dictionary** is spoken and then used in a simple sentence.

Mark went to the swimming pool
yesterday. He went with his father
and his sister, Cathy. He can swim
but his sister cannot.

Circle yes or no .

① Mark can swim.

yes
no

② Mark's sister can swim.

yes
no

③ Mark went to the swimming pool today.

yes
no

④ Mark went to the beach yesterday.

yes
no

⑤ Mark's father went to the swimming pool.

yes
no

⑥ Mark's father has black swimming shorts.

yes
no

⑦ The lifeguard is in the water.

yes
no

⑧ The lifeguard has a yellow shirt.

yes
no

Donna was not happy yesterday afternoon. She hurt her arm on the slide at the park. The nurse took an X-ray.

Complete the puzzle.

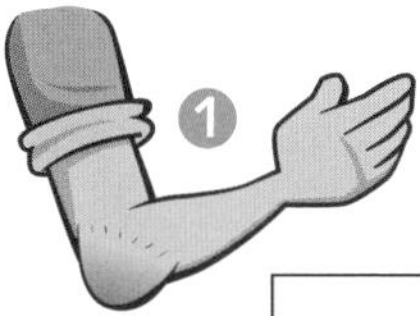

1				h	u	r	t
2			D				
3		u					
4							k
5						e	
6	d						
7					y		
8	g						

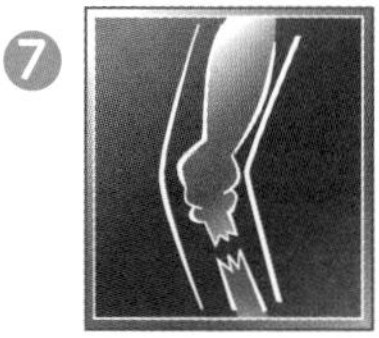

Look at the letters in pink. Where did Donna go yesterday? _ _ _ _ _ _ _ _

Donna's brother Martin didn't go to the hospital. He went to the train station to meet his Uncle Alan.

Rearrange the words.

❶ is Donna's brother Martin.
Martin is Donna's brother.

❷ go didn't the to hospital Martin.

❸ the station He to went train.

❹ Uncle is Alan Martin's.

❺ by came Alan Uncle train.

❻ his Martin went meet to uncle.

❼ arrived four The o'clock at train.

❽ happy see Alan to Martin was.

John went to the shops yesterday.
First he went to the bookstore.
Then he went to the post office.
He saw his friend Steve.

Find and write.

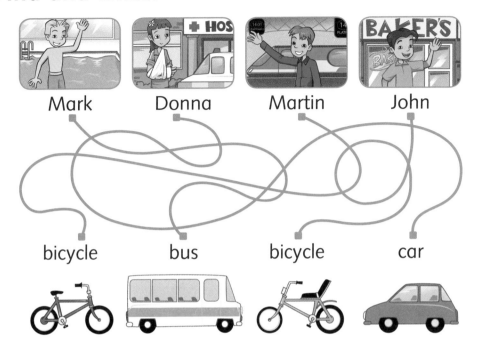

| Mark | Donna | Martin | John |

| bicycle | bus | bicycle | car |

❶ Mark went to the ___swimming pool___
by ___bus___ .

❷ Donna went to the _____
by _____ .

❸ Martin went to the _____
by _____ .

❹ John went to the _____
by _____ .

Kate went to the zoo with her friend
Rachel yesterday. They saw lions,
elephants, koalas, and monkeys.
Kate gave a banana to a monkey.

Write.

	elephant	monkey	lion	koala
big	✔		✔	
small		✔		✔
fast		✔	✔	
slow	✔			✔
cute		✔		✔
dangerous	✔		✔	

❶ Elephants are _____ big _____,

_____, and _____.

❷ Monkeys are _____,

_____, and _____.

❸ Lions _____ _____,

_____, and _____.

❹ _____ _____

_____, _____, and

_____.

11

Maria didn't go to the zoo
yesterday, she went to the library.
She likes to read. She took home
five books!

Complete your library card.

Newtown Library
468 Main Street, Newtown

DATE:

NAME:

MALE:

FEMALE:

DATE OF BIRTH:

AGE:

SCHOOL:

TELEPHONE NUMBER:

Tom and Rob went to a baseball game at the ballpark yesterday. The game was exciting. They ate hamburgers. They had fun!

1 Connect.

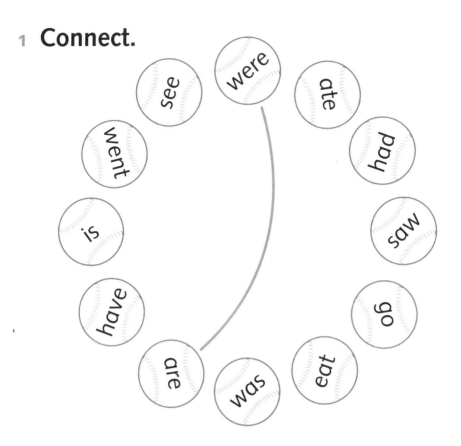

2 Complete. Use six words from the baseballs.

I ___had___ a good day yesterday. It

_____ a hot day. I _____ to

the supermarket and I _____ my

friend. We _____ hamburgers and

ice cream. We _____ very happy.

Clare didn't go to the baseball game. She was sick. She was at home in bed all day yesterday. Poor Clare!

Answer the questions.

❶ Where was Clare yesterday?

She was at home in bed.

❷ Where was Maria yesterday?

_____

❸ Where was Donna yesterday?

_____

❹ Where were Tom and Rob yesterday?

_____

❺ Where was Martin yesterday?

_____

❻ Where was Kate yesterday?

_____

❼ Where were you yesterday?

_____

Mike was at a restaurant with his family yesterday. It was his birthday. He had a big cake, and a lot of presents and cards.

Look at Mike's birthday party on page 18. Answer the questions.

❶ How many people are there? ___nine___

❷ How many boys are there? _____

❸ How old is Mike? _____

❹ How many cakes are there? _____

❺ How many birthday cards are there?

_____

❻ How many grandparents are there?

_____

❼ How many presents are there?

_____

❽ How many green presents are there?

_____

Amy was at the beach with her grandparents. They ate ice cream and drank soda. They made sandcastles. They played in the sea.

Rewrite. Use these words:

> she them she it he they
> them she it he it him

❶ Tom and Rob enjoyed the game .

They enjoyed it.

❷ Amy is with her grandparents .

_____

❸ John rode his bicycle to the shops.

_____

❹ Martin went to meet his uncle .

_____

❺ Donna doesn't like the hospital .

_____

❻ Maria took some books home.

_____

Amy's mother and father weren't at the beach yesterday. Her mother was at work in the hospital. Her father went to the office.

Can you remember? Complete the sentences.

❶ Mark went _to the swimming pool yesterday_.

❷ Donna hurt _____ .

❸ Kate and Rachel _____ .

❹ Maria _____ .

❺ Tom and Rob _____ .

❻ Mike _____ .

❼ Amy _____ .

Picture Dictionary

baseball

elbow

beach

elephant

card

hamburger

doctor

koala

lifeguard

sandcastle

lion

slide

monkey

swimming
pool

nurse

train
station

present

X-ray

25

Dolphin Readers

Dolphin Readers are available at five levels, from Starter to 4.

The Dolphins series covers four major themes:

Grammar, Living Together, The World Around Us, Science and Nature.

For each theme, there are two titles at every level.

Activity Books are available for all Dolphins.

All Dolphins are available on audio CD.
(2 TITLES ON EACH CD ⬭ SEE TABLE BELOW)

Teacher's Notes are available at **www.oup.com/elt/dolphins**

	Grammar	Living Together	The World Around Us	Science and Nature
Starter	• Silly Squirrel • Monkeying Around	• My Family • A Day with Baby	• Doctor, Doctor • Moving House	• A Game of Shapes • Baby Animals
Level 1	• Meet Molly • Where Is It?	• Little Helpers • Jack the Hero	• On Safari • Lost Kitten	• Number Magic • How's the Weather?
Level 2	• Double Trouble • Super Sam	• Candy for Breakfast • Lost!	• A Visit to the City • Matt's Mistake	• Numbers, Numbers Everywhere • Circles and Squares
Level 3	• Students in Space • What Did You Do Yesterday?	• New Girl in School • Uncle Jerry's Great Idea	• Just Like Mine • Wonderful Wild Animals	• Things That Fly • Let's Go to the Rainforest
Level 4	• The Tough Task • Yesterday, Today, and Tomorrow	• We Won the Cup • Up and Down	• Where People Live • City Girl, Country Boy	• In the Ocean • Go, Gorillas, Go